W9-AAW-768

Ripley's Believe It or Not!

Believe It or Not!

WEIRD-ITIES!

Publisher Anne Marshall
Editorial Director Rebecca Miles
Assistant Editor Charlotte Howell
Text Geoff Tibballs
Proofreader Judy Barratt
Picture Researchers James Proud, Charlotte Howell
Indexer Hilary Bird
Art Director Sam South
Senior Designer Michelle Foster
Reprographics Juice Creative

Executive Vice President Norm Deska
Vice President, Archives and Exhibits Edward Meyer

PUBLISHER'S NOTE

While every effort has been made to verify the accuracy of the entries in this book, the Publishers cannot be held responsible for any errors contained in the work. They would be glad to receive any information from readers.

WARNING

Some of the stunts and activities in this book are undertaken by experts and should not be attempted by anyone without adequate training and supervision.

Published by Ripley Publishing 2013
Ripley Publishing, Suite 188, 7576 Kingspointe Parkway, Orlando, Florida 32819, USA

2 4 6 8 10 9 7 5 3 1

Copyright © 2013 by Ripley Entertainment Inc.
All rights reserved. Ripley's Believe It or Not!, and Ripley's, Believe It or Not! are registered trademarks of Ripley Entertainment Inc.

ISBN 978-1-60991-021-1

Some of this material first appeared in *Ripley's Believe It or Not! Expect... The Unexpected*

Library Of Congress Cataloging-in-Publication data is available.

Manufactured in China in July/2013
1st printing

No part of this publication may be reproduced in whole or in part, or stored in a retrieval system, or transmitted in any form or by any means, electronic, mechanical, photocopying, recording, or otherwise, without written permission from the publisher. For information regarding permission, write to VP Intellectual Property, Ripley Entertainment Inc., Suite 188, 7576 Kingspointe Parkway, Orlando, Florida 32819
email publishing@ripleys.com

Ripley's Believe It or Not!

WEIRD-ITIES!

IMPOSSIBLE FEATS

Ripley
PUBLISHING

a Jim Pattison Company

PAGE
32

PAGE
40

U.S. POST OFFICE
ECHO UTAH 84024

IMPOSSIBLE FEATS

You won't believe it. A collection of rare stunts, bizarre feats, and incredible performers will stun and surprise you. Discover the man who swallows everything from light bulbs to live goldfish, the woman who can blow up a hot water bottle until it bursts, and the surfer who caught a 70-ft (21.3-m) wave.

PAGE 43

PAGE 47

ICE BREAKER

Lewis Pugh combines extreme swimming with Polar adventure. Besides being the first person to complete a long-distance swim in all five oceans of the world, British swimmer Pugh has also completed the most southern swim ever undertaken, earning him the name "The Ice Bear."

Wearing only swimming shorts, goggles, and a cap, Pugh plunged into the freezing sea off the Antarctic Peninsula in December 2005 to swim 0.6 mi (1 km) in a water temperature of only 32°F (0°C). To reach the spot just below the 65th parallel off Petermann Island, an ice-breaker ship had to cut through 25 mi (40 km) of thick pack-ice. Although it was dusk and snowing heavily, Pugh decided to undertake the swim on the night of December 14 before the ice closed over again.

The swim was undertaken on the 94th anniversary of the Norwegian explorer Roald Amundsen becoming the first man to reach the South Pole.

This incredible feat took Pugh 18 minutes 10 seconds. He said, "As soon as I dived in, I had a screaming pain all over my body. After three minutes, I'd lost all feeling in my hands and feet, and after six minutes I lost all feeling throughout my arms and legs. I am not sure how I kept on going for so long. I had to concentrate all the time and swim as fast as I could to keep the cold out. I am ecstatic to have swum so close to the South Pole."

Thirty-five-year-old Pugh enjoys pushing back boundaries, many of which, he says, are ultimately mental rather than physical.

Before Pugh entered the water, he was able to raise his core body temperature to 101.1°F (38.4°C) without doing anything other than looking at the icy water.

FISH SCHOOL

Dean and Kyle Pomerleau teach fish to perform tricks. Sir Isaac Newton, the Betta Fish pictured here, learned to go through a hoop after a week of training.

QUICK ON THE DRAW

German artist Gero Hilliger can produce portraits faster than a Polaroid camera. He is able to complete a portrait in just over six seconds and once rattled out 384 in 90 minutes. He can also do portraits blindfolded—purely by touch.

SAW BIKE

In 2004, a German inventor came up with the Dolmette, a huge superbike powered by 24 chainsaws.

TEN-YEAR TRIP

Argentina's Emilio Scotto rode 457,000 mi (735,500 km) on a motorcycle between 1985 and 1995. He went round the world twice and visited more than 200 countries.

SHARK RIDER

Fearless Manny Puig isn't content with getting right up close to sharks—he rides them, too! He follows hammerhead sharks in a boat off Florida Keys, then leaps on them and hangs on while they thrash about in the water. He even tackles more dangerous bull sharks, grabbing them by two holes near the gills before climbing on. Manny also dives into swamps in the Everglades and rides alligators with his bare hands. He says: "I rely on proper technique and the grace of God."

STUNT KID

When he was just 2½ years old and still wearing diapers, Evan Wasser was an American skateboarding ace! Riding a skateboard that was almost as tall as he was, he could perform amazing jump stunts.

MIGHTY MOLARS

A 71-year-old Chinese woman pulled a car a distance of 65 ft (19 m) in 2005—with her teeth. Wang Xiaobei attached one end of a heavy rope to the car and wrapped a handkerchief around the other end before biting on the rope. Among other items she can carry in her mouth are a 55-lb (25-kg) bucket of water and a bicycle.

COURAGEOUS SWIM

In September 2001, Ashley Cowan, aged 15, from Toronto, Ontario, became the youngest person and first disabled athlete to swim across Lake Erie. She managed to complete the 12-mi (19-km) swim in 14 hours, despite having had all four limbs amputated below the joints when she had meningitis as an infant.

MINI RIDER

In 2003, Swede Tom Wiberg constructed a mini motorcycle that was just 2½ in (6.4 cm) high and 4½ in (11.4 cm) long. It had a top speed of 1.2 mph (1.9 km/h), thanks to a minuscule, ethanol-powered combustion engine.

EAR POWER

A Chinese man is able to blow up balloons and blow out candles with his ears. Wei Mingtang, from Guilin City, discovered more than 30 years ago that his ears leaked, after which he came up with the idea of using them to inflate balloons with the aid of a pipe. And he once blew out 20 candles in a line in just 20 seconds using a hose attached to his ears.

SPEEDY SEVENTY

Ed Whitlock, aged 72, of Toronto, Ontario, Canada, became the first person over the age of 70 to run a marathon in under three hours.

MONSTER JUMP

Driving monster truck Bigfoot 14, Dan Runte, from St. Louis, Missouri, jumped 202 ft (62 m) over a Boeing 727 airplane at Smyrna Airport, Tennessee, in 1999.

JOE'S JAUNTS

Aged 62, Joe Bowen made his third trip across the U.S. He became famous in 1967 when he cycled 14,000 mi (22,530 km) on a winding route from California to his home in eastern Kentucky. Then, in 1980, he walked on stilts from Los Angeles, California, to Powell County, Kentucky, on a more direct route. It took him six months to plod more than 3,000 mi (4,828 km) through driving rain and desert heat. And, in 2005, he retraced his original cycle route, this time with 58 lb (26.3 kg) of equipment strapped to his bike.

THE ICE MAN SWIMMETH

Dutchman Wim Hof says that, like fish, his body contains a form of antifreeze. In 2000, he swam 187 ft (57 m) under ice in a lake near Kolari, Finland, wearing only trunks and goggles. Then, in 2004, he spent 1 hour 8 minutes in direct, full-body contact with ice.

INSTANT BEAUTY

"One-minute beautician" Uma Jayakumar can create a hairstyle using a hairpin in seven seconds. In July 2005, the Indian hairdresser created 66 hairstyles in a minute, using a chopstick.

BOAT PULL

At the age of 65, Maurice Catarcio, from Middle Township, New Jersey, swam the backstroke while tugging an 80-ft (24-m) sightseeing boat across a lake. And at 72, the former wrestler dragged a 27,000-lb (12,247-kg) bus down a New York City street.

LOOK, NO HANDS!

At the 2002 X-games, Mat Hoffman, a 30-year-old BMX bike rider from Oklahoma City, performed the first no-handed 900, where the bike goes through 2½ spins.

COLD COMFORT

Gilberto Cruz remained buried in ice for 1 hour 6 minutes 24 seconds at a Brazilian shopping center in 2005. The 42-year-old performed the stunt in a transparent box in the mall at Ribeirao Preto with only his head sticking out of the ice.

RELIGIOUS VISION

Indian sculptor Rama Satish Shah makes intricate models of religious figures, while blindfolded. Over the past five years, she has created 36,000 figures from plaster of Paris, ranging in height from ¼ in (½ cm) to 9 in (23 cm). Each one takes her about 3 minutes to make.

CAST ADRIFT

Fishermen Lafaili Tofi and Telea Pa'a, from Western Samoa, survived for six months after drifting 2,480 mi (3,990 km) in the Pacific Ocean in a small metal boat.

CAMEL VAULTING

At the 2004 Yemeni Traditional Sports Festival, Ahmed Abdullah al-Abrash was crowned world camel-jumping champion after using a trampoline to vault over a line of camels 10 ft (3 m) long.

WORLD TREK

On June 20, 1970, brothers David and John Kunst set off from their hometown of Waseca, Minnesota, aiming to become the first people to walk around the world. Four years, 3 months, and 21 pairs of shoes later, David completed the 14,450-mi (23,255-km) trek (he flew across the oceans), arriving back in Waseca with mixed emotions. Sadly, his brother had been killed by bandits in Afghanistan only halfway through the expedition.

ALL OF A QUIVER

Terry Bryan, from Colorado Springs, caught an arrow traveling 135-mph (217-km/h) with his bare hands on an edition of the *Ripley's Believe It or Not!* TV show. Not only did he successfully complete the challenge, he went on to do it again—blindfolded!

BIT BY BAT

Jeanna Giese, of Wisconsin, became the first documented person to survive rabies without being given a vaccination! The 15-year-old girl was bitten by a bat in September 2004.

CHOPPER BIKE

Believe it or not, Las Vegas stunt rider Johnny Airtime once jumped his motorcycle over the spinning blades of four helicopters!

SPEED JUMPING

Forty-seven-year-old Jay Stokes, from Arizona, made no fewer than 534 successful parachute jumps in 24 hours at Lake Elsinore, California, in November 2003. With the help of three pilots working in two planes in rotating two-to three-hour shifts, he was able to average just under 2 minutes 45 seconds per run.

HOT BREATH

Tipnis Shobha, from India, is able to blow up a regular hot-water bottle until it bursts. Shobha accomplished her incredible feat in Germany in 2005.

TOP-HEAVY

Johnny Eck was born in Baltimore without the lower portion of his body. He got around by walking on his hands, as seen in this photo, taken in 1937.

ON TARGET

Darts player Perry Prine, from Mentor, Ohio, threw 1,432 bull's-eyes in 10 hours in March 1998. In that time, he threw a total of 6,681 darts—that is 11 darts a minute, of which on average 2.39 were bull's-eyes. He calculated that in the 10 hours, he walked more than 3 mi (5 km) to and from the dart board.

INDIAN TRAIL

A Hungarian immigrant now based in Edgewater, Florida, 58-year-old Peter Wolf Toth traveled the U.S. from 1971 to 1988, carving faces into logs in each state. Sculptor Toth enjoys carving images of American Indians—so much so that his 67 towering statues (some as tall as 40 ft/12 m high) can be found in every U.S. state, as well as in Canada. This "Trail of Whispering Giants" stretches from Desert Hot Springs in California to Springfield, Massachusetts.

LONG THROW

Believe it or not, the magician and card-trick specialist Rick Smith Jr., of Cleveland, Ohio, can throw a playing card a distance of 216 ft (66 m)!

INSTANT ART

Using only a palette knife and wads of toilet tissue, "Instant Artist" Morris Katz has created and sold over 225,000 original oil paintings in a 50-year

BRICK LIFT

Eighty-seven-year-old Xie Tianzhuang, from China, lifted 14 bricks, weighing a total of 77 lb (35 kg), with his teeth, in Hefei in October 2005. He managed to hold the bricks suspended for 15 seconds.

career. In July 1987, he painted for 12 consecutive hours at a hotel in his native New York City, during which time he finished 103 paintings and sold 55 on the spot. He once painted a 12 x 16 in (30 x 40 cm) canvas of a child in the snow in just 30 seconds.

SUPER SIZE

Isaac "Dr. Size" Nesser, of Greensburg, Pennsylvania, started lifting weights at the tender age of eight. As a result, it's perhaps of little surprise that he ended up boasting a 74-in (188-cm) chest, 29-in (74-cm) biceps, and the ability to bench press a massive 825 lb (374 kg). And if you ever need someone to carry 100-gal (380-l) drums filled with gas, Dr. Size is definitely the man for the job.

SHALLOW LEAP

A 34-year-old Indian policeman, R. Velmurugan, jumped from a height of 34 ft (10 m) into a tub containing just 7 in (18 cm) of water in 2005.

SUPER SURFER

Pete Cabrinha of Hawaii surfed a 70-ft (21.3-m) wave at the break known as Jaws on the North Shore of Maui, Hawaii, on January 10, 2004.

It was the largest wave ever ridden at the Global Big Wave Awards. Cabrinha set off to practice on a brand-new board to warm up before the event, but ended up surfing in on this staggering wave.

MARATHON MISSION

Margaret Hagerty has run a marathon on each of the Earth's seven continents—quite an achievement for a woman of 81. The elderly athlete, from Concord, North Carolina, completed her mission by taking part in Australia's Gold Coast Marathon in 2004, having previously run in locations including Greece, Brazil, and the South Pole. Asked how long she will keep going, she said: "Some days I think I am going to pick a date, run, and quit. But then I think, 'Well, they can just pick me up off the street one day.'"

ACTION MAN

Although born without arms, Jim Goldman, from St. Louis, Missouri, can play baseball by placing the bat between his neck and shoulder. Using this method, he can hit a 60-mph (97-km/h) fastball thrown by a semi-pro ball player.

SPINNING AROUND

Suspended 525 ft (160 m) above the Rhine River, Germany, two German tightrope artists made a spectacular motorcycle river crossing in 2003. The bike was connected to a trapeze dangling beneath the high wire. Johann Traber sat on the trapeze, while his son, 19-year-old Johann, rode the motorcycle. They spun around the wire 14 times during the 1,900-ft (579-m) crossing, using shifts in their weight to keep revolving.

QUEST

For more than eight years, Rafael Antonio Lozano has been making his way across North America—as part of his mission to visit every Starbucks coffee shop on the planet. By September 2005, the 33-year-old coffee lover from Houston, Texas (who uses the name Winter), had visited an incredible 4,886 Starbucks shops in North America and 213 in other countries including Spain, England, France, and Japan. His record for a single day was visiting 29 shops in southern California.

BAR-TAILED GODWIT

The bar-tailed godwit is a migratory bird that would be hard to beat in an endurance flying contest—it migrates 7,456 mi (12,000 km) from Alaska to New Zealand in six days and six nights at speeds of up to 56 mph (90 km/h) without stopping to feed.

THE HIGH LIFE

Walking a tightrope 300 ft (91 m) above ground would be scary enough for most people, but Jay Cochrane has done it blindfolded! In 1998, Cochrane, from Toronto, Ontario, Canada, walked 600 ft (184 m) between the towers of the Flamingo Hilton, Las Vegas. Known as the "Prince of the Air," Cochrane once spent 21 days on a high wire in Puerto Rico. In 1995, he walked a tightrope 2,098 ft (639 m) above the Yangtze River in China, and in 2001 he walked 2,190 ft (667 m) between two 40-story buildings on opposite sides of the Love River in the city of Kaohsiung in Taiwan.

WHEELIE HIGH

In July 1998, Super Joe Reed made a 65-ft (20-m) leap on a 250cc dirtbike from the roof of one building to another in Los Angeles, California. The roofs were 140 ft (43 m) above street level.

IN FATHER'S FOOTSTEPS

U.S. motorcycle stuntman Robbie Knievel (son of the famous daredevil Evel Knievel) made a spectacular 180-ft (55-m) jump over two helicopters and five airplanes parked on the deck of the Intrepid Museum, Manhattan, New York, in 2004. He had to construct a ski ramp 30 ft (9 m) high to help the motorbike build up enough speed to clear the aircraft-carrier-turned-museum.

LUG TUG

A Chinese man can pull a train with his ear! Thirty-nine-year-old Zhang Xinquan pulled a 24-ton train 130 ft (40 m) along a track in June 2005 by means of a chain attached to his right ear. After years of practice, he admits that his right ear is now bigger than his left. The previous month he had pulled a car 65 ft (20 m) with both ears while walking on eggs, without breaking them. The father of 15 children can also stand on eggs and pick up a 55-lb (25-kg) bicycle with his mouth.

BLIND CORNERS

Blindfolded and with a hood over his head, 19-year-old Samartha Shenoy, from India, rode a motor scooter for 15 mi (24 km) through the streets of Mangalore in 2004.

FLYING VISIT

In May 2004, Geoff Marshall traveled to all 275 stations on the London Underground system in just 18 hours 35 minutes 43 seconds.

MOONWALK RELAY

In October 2002, a relay team comprising Adam Hall, Ramsey Brookhart, and Joshua Dodd moonwalked 30 mi (48 km) from Boulder, Colorado, to Denver.

JUGGLING HEAVYWEIGHT

Believe it or not, Bob Whitcomb, from Ohio, juggles bowling balls. He can catch three 16-lb (7.3-kg) balls 62 consecutive times.

HUNGRY EYES

This pine snake, found in Gainesville, Florida, was discovered in a chicken coop after having eaten two light bulbs he mistook for eggs. The bulbs were three times the size of the snake's head and would have been fatal, but for a successful operation to have them removed.

CABLE CAR SURVIVAL

On March 16, 2004, in Singapore, 36 teams of two took up the challenge of surviving seven days inside a cable car. They were allowed only one 10-minute toilet break each day. Nineteen of the couples survived the challenge, emerging on April 23 after experiencing 168 hours of stifling humidity, motion sickness, and claustrophobic conditions.

SLICE OF LUCK

When veterinarian Jon-Paul Carew looked at this X ray he could hardly believe his eyes—a puppy aged 6 months had somehow swallowed a 13-in (33-cm) serrated knife!

Jane Scarola had been using a knife to carve a turkey at her home in Plantation, Florida, in September 2005. She put the blade on the counter away from the edge, but thinks that one of her six other dogs must have snatched it. From there it came into the possession of Elsie, her inquisitive St. Bernard puppy, who swallowed it! Elsie probably had the blade between her esophagus and stomach for four days before Dr. Carew removed it in an operation lasting two hours.

Dr. Carew admitted: "I was just amazed that a dog this small could take down a knife that big and not do any serious damage, and be as bright, alert, and happy as she was."

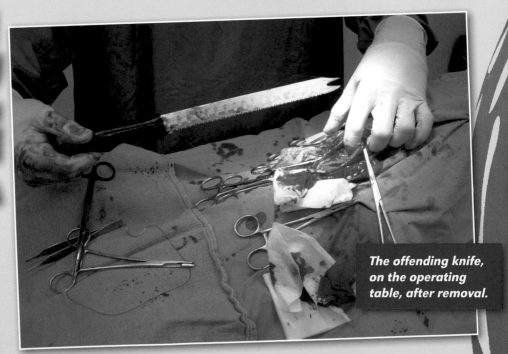

The offending knife, on the operating table, after removal.

X ray of the knife lying between Elsie's esophagus and stomach.

Jon-Paul Carew with Elsie after her operation to remove the knife.

21

GRAPE CATCH

In 1991, in the town of East Boston, Massachusetts, Paul J. Tavilla, who is known as "The Grape Catcher," incredibly caught a grape in his mouth after it had been thrown by James Dealy from a distance of 327 ft 6 in (99.8 m).

MARATHON PUSH

Rob Kmet and A.J. Zeglen, from Winnipeg, Manitoba, pushed a 2,600-lb (1,180-kg) sports car 43 mi (70 km) around Winnipeg's Gimli racetrack in 2005. At the end of the 24-hour push, the two men were hardly able to walk.

CLIMBING GRANNY

When 78-year-old grandmother Nie Sanmei accidentally locked herself out of her fifth-floor apartment in Changsha, China, in 2005, she started scaling the outside of the building! Using window grills as handholds

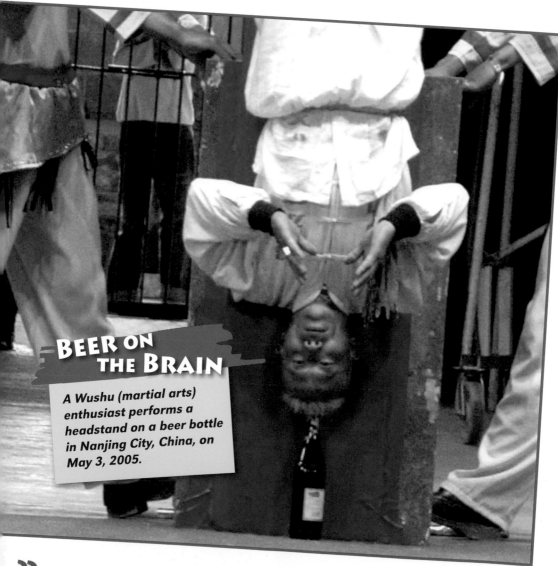

BEER ON THE BRAIN

A Wushu (martial arts) enthusiast performs a headstand on a beer bottle in Nanjing City, China, on May 3, 2005.

and footholds, she reached the fourth floor before her concerned daughter-in-law arrived with the key.

CAR JUMP

Believe it or not, Andy Macdonald once jumped over four cars on a skateboard! He made the jump of 52 ft 10 in (16.1 m) at East Lansing, Michigan, in 1999.

BLIND RACER

Blind motorcyclist Mike Newman, from Manchester, England, raced a powerful 1,000cc motorbike at speeds of up to 89 mph (143 km/h), guided only by radio instructions!

MOUTH CONTROL

Despite having no movement in her arms and legs, a British woman, Hilary Lister, was able to sail solo across the English Channel in August 2005 by steering her boat, Malin, with her mouth. Aged 33, Hilary controlled the boat by sucking and blowing on two plastic tubes connected to pressure switches that operated the tiller and sails. She navigated the 21-mi (34-km) voyage from Dover, England, to Calais, France, in a specially modified keelboat in 6 hours 13 minutes.

TOOTH AND NAIL

Georges Christen, is one of the world's strongest men. He can stop a plane from taking off with his teeth, pull trains, bend nails, and power a Ferris wheel—but insists he is a gentle giant.

IN DEPTH

What inspired you to become one of the world's strongest men?

"As a child in Luxembourg, I was fascinated by circus strongmen. Aged 16, I started lifting weights, and then I saw a French guy on television bending 50 iron carpenter's nails. I broke his record by bending 250 with my teeth when I was 19."

What are your most famous stunts?

"I prevented three 110-horsepower Cessna Sport airplanes from taking off at full power—one with my teeth and two with my arms. I have also pulled trucks, buses, railway carriages, and a 95,000-kg ship—all with my teeth. At Luxembourg's Schobermesse fair, I made a 45-m, 60,000-kg Ferris wheel turn by pulling it with a rope by my teeth. And I like tearing telephone books—I can rip 1,344-page books into several pieces."

Are your stunts dangerous?

"A favorite is blowing up a hot-water bottle until it bursts—the pressure could blow back into my lungs and kill me. But I train and calculate the risks."

So how do you train—and how do you protect your teeth?

"I train every day—a mixture of physical strength and mental concentration to liberate all the force you need at one special moment. My teeth aren't perfect—when I was about 20, my dentist told me not to use my teeth in this way, but I did anyway and now he often comes to my shows because I'm good publicity for him! I used to work for an insurance company, but they won't insure me because they have no way of knowing how dangerous it is to prevent a plane taking off."

What is the most difficult stunt to do?

"I can now bend 368 nails in one hour. And, although it's not as spectacular, the hardest one is tearing a deck of 120 playing cards, because they are small and hard to grip, and also because they are plastic-coated."

How do you think of new stunts?

"I have a collection of books and posters of old-time strongmen, and I try to adapt their stunts for modern times. If they were holding back horses, I make it airplanes. I might lift a table with my teeth—and have a woman sitting on top."

Has your strength ever got you into trouble?

"I try not to be a strongman in my private life—if people want to pick a fight, I tell them it's just my job. I once accidentally pulled the bumper off a car at a car show. And I also once unintentionally broke a 'test your strength' machine at a fairground."

How long will you carry on testing your strength?

"I taught the telephone-book stunt to my office-worker father, and he was still doing it when he was 94! I have bought an old blacksmith's forge and I'm turning it into a small museum full of things strongmen used to use and wear. People can come and train the way they did. My main vision now is to entertain."

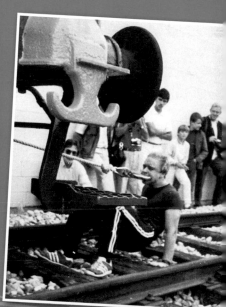

WALKING ON AIR

An Uygur tightrope walker spent a long 37 days and nights living on a 100-ft (30-m) high wire stretched across a dam in Nanjing, China, in May 2005. Thirty-two-year-old Aisikaier comes from a family of high-wire walkers, and had spent 26 days on a wire in 2004, but this time he managed to stay up longer. He spent his nights in a makeshift shelter attached to the thick wire. To kill time and alleviate the boredom during the day, he performed daring hula-hoop, unicycle, and balancing tricks. The only contact he had with the world below was via his cell phone, which he used so that he could answer questions about his feat, or talk to fans.

DOUG'S DELIGHT

In 2005, at the end of a 25-year marathon, Doug Slaughter, from Greentown, Indiana, finally achieved his goal of cycling 25,000 non-road mi (40,230 km). Doug had always wanted to bike the distance of the world's circumference, but because he was born with a mild handicap, he has never cycled on a road. Instead, he rode on driveways, parking lots, and forest trails, using an odometer to track his progress. He also used a stationary bike to cover some of the distance. Having achieved that target, Doug has no intention of stopping there: he's now aiming for 50,000 mi (80,465 km).

SPORTING DOUBLE

In October 2003, just 22 hours after making a hole-in-one at Pleasant View Golf Course, Paul Hughes, 74, of Waunakee, Wisconsin, bowled a 300 game at Middleton, Wisconsin.

IN THE DARK

Teenage bowling champion Amy Baker, from Houston, Texas, has an unusual recipe for success—she practices blindfolded. As soon as she started bowling wearing a dark eyemask—at the suggestion of her coach Jim Sands—her scores improved dramatically, enabling her to become a national champion.

BACKWARDS BOB

Known to his friends as "Backwards Bob," Canada's Bob Gray can write backward and upside down with both hands simultaneously. He can also spell backward phonetically.

MS. DYNAMITE

Protected by only a helmet and a flimsy costume, American entertainer Allison Bly has blown herself up more than 1,500 times with explosives equivalent to the force of two sticks of dynamite. "The Dynamite Lady" performs the stunt inside a box she calls the "Coffin of Death," but has so far suffered nothing worse than broken bones, concussion, and powder burns.

YOUNG SOLDIER

Calvin Graham, the youngest U.S. serviceman in World War II, was wounded in combat, then later discharged for lying about his age—he was only 12 years old.

FANTASTIC FEET

Claudia Gomez, of Baton Rouge, Louisiana, can use her feet to shoot a bull's-eye with a bow and arrow while doing a handstand!

JUGGLING JOGGER

Believe it or not, 33-year-old Michal Kapral, from Toronto, Ontario, ran a marathon in 3 hours 7 minutes in September 2005 while juggling three balls at the same time!

WALKING ON WATER

When Rémy Bricka first crossed the Atlantic in 1972, it was on board a luxury liner. For his second Atlantic crossing—16 years later—he decided to walk! The Frenchman set off from the Canary Islands on April 2, 1988, with his feet lashed to 14-ft (4.3-m) fiberglass pontoons. Behind him he towed a raft that contained a coffin-sized sleeping compartment, a compass, and water desalinators. He took no food, eating only plankton and the occasional flying fish that landed on his raft. Walking 50 mi (80 km) a day, he reached Trinidad on May 31, highly emaciated, and hallucinating, at the end of his 3,502-mi (5,636-km) hike across the ocean.

MULE TRAIN

Desperate to attend a 2005 Mule Days festival in Ralston, Wyoming, Pam Fedirchuck and Tara Lewis reckoned the only way to get there from their home in Rocky Mountain House, Alberta, was by mule. Riding two mules and leading a third that carried supplies, they made the 857-mi (1,380-km) trip in 52 days.

OLDEST ACE

Aged 101, Harold Stilson became the oldest golfer to make a hole-in-one when he landed an ace at the 16th hole at Deerfield Country Club, Florida, in May 2001. A 27-handicap golfer, he started playing at the age of 20, but did not make the first of his six holes-in-one until he was 71.

KARAOKE KING

Barry Yip, a D.J. from Hong Kong, spent 81 hours 23 seconds singing 1,000 karaoke songs.

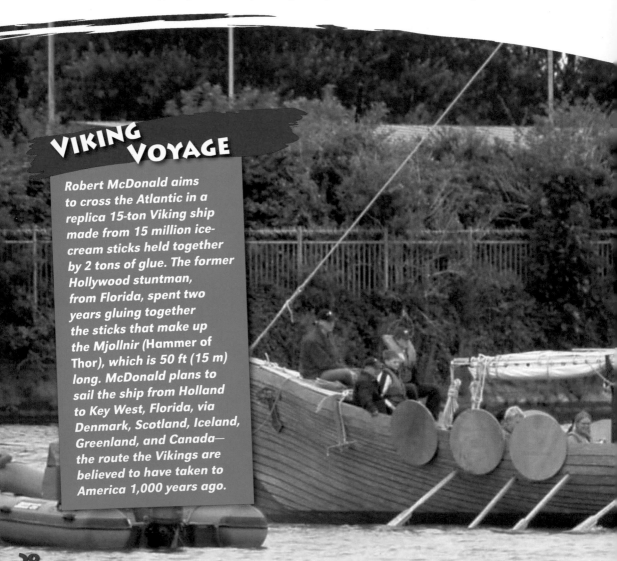

VIKING VOYAGE

Robert McDonald aims to cross the Atlantic in a replica 15-ton Viking ship made from 15 million ice-cream sticks held together by 2 tons of glue. The former Hollywood stuntman, from Florida, spent two years gluing together the sticks that make up the Mjollnir (Hammer of Thor), which is 50 ft (15 m) long. McDonald plans to sail the ship from Holland to Key West, Florida, via Denmark, Scotland, Iceland, Greenland, and Canada—the route the Vikings are believed to have taken to America 1,000 years ago.

MARITAL BLISS

Zhang Jiuyu and Guo Changlan celebrate their marriage of 80 years 15 days in Shijiazhuang, China, on October 23, 2005. The 96-year-old couple have one child, three grandchildren, and three great-grandchildren.

SHARP PRACTICE

The daredevil ethnic games that took place in Guiyang, southwest China, in May 2005, were certainly at the cutting edge of sport.

This performer can be seen swallowing a red-hot sword as spectators look on.

The Miao people, whose favorite pastime is buffalo fighting, used the games to demonstrate their expertise at such feats as swallowing a red-hot sword and walking barefoot on the razor-sharp blade of a giant knife. Children got in on the act too, with a 13-year-old girl balancing delicately on the tips of knives. The opening ceremony was also a far cry from the Olympics, a group of Miao kung-fu artists performing a series of amazing stunts.

Standing on broken glass and walking on a series of knife points are two of the amazing feats in these unusual games.

Instead of using his hands, this man is swinging bricks around using his chest. They are tied to a needle that pierces his body.

INCREDIBLE HUNK

Although he weighed only 88 lb (40 kg) at the age of 16, Dennis Rogers, from Houston, Texas, could lift twice his body weight over his head! Once the smallest boy in his class, Rogers, who weighs in at 160 lb (72.5 kg), is pound-for-pound the strongest man in the world. He can tear thick books vertically using only two fingers and can bend a solid steel bar around his neck into a U-shape. In 1995, he successfully prevented four Harley Davidson Sportster motorcycles, powered at full throttle, from moving for 12 seconds.

SWEET CATCH

One of the weirdest acts on the U.S. entertainment circuit features Scott Jeckel blowing marshmallows from his nose into the mouth of Ray Perisin, who then swallows them. The Illinois pair started performing their act with popcorn, but switched to marshmallows, as they were more aerodynamic.

STAIR CRAZY

Most people would take the elevator up an apartment block, but not Bernadette Hallfeld Duychak. She's crazy about climbing stairs! In August 2005, she climbed Harbor Point—her 54-storey condominium in downtown Chicago, Illinois—more than 55 times in 24 hours, making a total of around 40,000 stairs. "When I started, I could barely climb 20 floors. Now I climb at least 2,000 floors a week!"

EGG-HEAD

New Yorker Barnaby Ruhe can throw a boomerang on a 100-ft (30-m) elliptical path so that it returns to hit an egg that he has carefully placed on top of his own head! Ruhe has made more than 100 successful hits and has been whacked only a few times. He says of his eggsploits: "What you throw out is what you get back."

IRON BEAR

Harold "Chief Iron Bear" Collins, from Shannon, North Carolina, pulled a 22.87-ton truck 100 ft (30 m) in under 40 seconds in New York City in 1999. A full-blooded Lumbee Native American, Collins is certainly built for the part: He has a 63-in (160-cm) chest.

EGG CATCHER

Brad Freeman didn't end up with egg on his face in 2005. Instead, the 25-year-old from Calgary, Alberta, caught a boiled egg in his mouth thrown from an amazing distance of 275 ft (84 m).

BIRD MAN OF DEVON

When Jonathan Marshall goes hang gliding near his home, in Devon, England, he not only flies like a bird—he flies with birds. He has trained wild birds to join him in flight. Marshall became obsessed with the idea of flying with birds when he was eight years old and has spent the past decade training a few falcons to fly with him. "Flying with birds puts you right into their world," he says. "Up there, flying at 1,000 ft (305 m), I see everything from their point of view. How many people have that experience?"

EYE-BLOWING FEAT

By forcing air out of the tear ducts in his eyes, Alfred Langevin, of Detroit, was able to blow up balloons and smoke, and even blow out candles.

STRONG TEETH

Sam Marlow, of Chelsea, Massachusetts, could lift a barrel of beer weighing 260 lb (118 kg) with his teeth while also performing a handstand.

HANDICAP GOLFER

A Florida golfer achieved three holes-in-one over a 6-month period—all while swinging one-handed! Sixty-eight-year-old Bill Hilsheimer, from Nokomis, lost most of his right hand in a childhood accident, and uses only his left arm when he swings. But after waiting 50 years for his first ace, he racked up three between September 2003 and March 2004. The odds of an amateur golfer hitting a hole-in-one are 12,600 to 1. The odds of Bill's incredible feat would be impossible to calculate.

HUMAN CARTOON

New Yorker Rob Lok is known as "The Human Cartoon" because he is able to smash a watermelon with his head!

BIKER MARATHON

In May 2002, British couple Simon and Monika Newbound set off from Dublin, Ireland, on a monumental motorcycle journey that would take them more than three years. By May 2005, the pair had clocked up visits to 54 countries and had ridden an amazing 105,000 mi (169,000 km). As well as circumnavigating the world, they rode north of the Arctic Circle three times on three different continents, crossed the U.S. from coast to coast five times, and visited every U.S. state and Canadian province. During their mammoth journey they rode 1,600 mi (2,600 km) off-road

EAR-LIFTING

Zafar Gill, from Pakistan, lifted an ear-bending 121 lb (55 kg) and held them for 12.22 seconds suspended from one of his ears! He successfully completed this amazing feat in Germany, in November 2005.

in Mongolia, had an audience with the Pope in Rome, and camped on the Great Wall of China.

GLOBE TROTTER

In three years of travel between 2000 and 2003, Charles Veley visited a staggering 350 countries, enclaves, islands, federations, and territories, spending over $1 million on journeying almost a million miles. His most difficult destination was Clipperton Island, a remote French territory 700 mi (1,126 km) off the coast of Mexico in the Pacific Ocean. Owing to a treacherous reef, his boat was unable to land, forcing him to swim to shore. "There was nothing else I could do," he smiles. "By then I was obsessed with completing my goal."

EAR PIERCER

Jill Drake, of Kent, England, won a contest for the loudest screamer, with a scream of 129 decibels—that's as loud as a pneumatic drill.

HARD TO SWALLOW

Stevie Starr, from Scotland, is a professional regurgitator. He swallows such objects as light bulbs, coins, live goldfish, and glass eyes before bringing them back up again.

Stevie also swallows butane and soap, and then blows out a gas-filled bubble. He swallows a ring and locked padlock—when the articles are returned, the ring is locked inside the padlock! When Stevie swallows numbered coins, he can retrieve them at will, and in whichever order the audience requests.

He learned his talent while living in a children's home in Glasgow, Scotland. "I used to swallow pennies to hide them from the other kids... I didn't realize that someday I'd be doing it for a living."

Stevie regurgitates dry sugar after having previously swallowed a bowlful with a glass of water.

Having swallowed the goldfish with plenty of water, Stevie safely retrieves them.

GRAN TOUR

A Californian grandmother completed a journey down the west coast of North America in 2002, riding solo on an 11-ft (3.4-m) watercraft. Jane Usatin, 56, from Carlsbad, set off from Blaine, Washington, and reached Mexico 28 travel-days later at the end of a 1,828-mi (2,941-km) trip.

BALL TOWER

In November 1998, David Kremer, of Waukesha, Wisconsin, stacked ten bowling balls vertically without using any adhesive.

AMERICAN ODYSSEY

In June 2005, Jason Hill climbed on his bike in Deadhorse, Alaska, and began pedaling. By January 2006, he had reached Missoula, Montana, but his ultimate destination is Tierra del Fuego in Argentina. He reckons the 19,000-mi (30,600-km) journey, all the way from the Arctic Circle to the very bottom of South America, will take him more than two years.

BLINDING SPEED

In September 2005, Hein Wagner, 33, of Cape Town, South Africa, drove a car at a speed of 168 mph (270 km)—even though he has been blind since birth.

PACIFIC CROSSING

Steve Fisher, from Toledo, Ohio, crossed the Pacific Ocean from California to Hawaii in 1997 on a 17-ft (5.2-m) windsurfer. The 2,612-mi (4,200-km) journey on *Da Slippa II* took him 47 days.

MEXICAN WAVE

An amazing 42 Brazilian surfers rode a small wave together on Macumba Beach in Rio de Janeiro on November 18, 2005.

ESCAPE ARTIST

Queensland-based escape artist Ben Bradshaw managed to free himself from a straitjacket while fully submerged in a tank of water in just 38.59 seconds in Sydney, Australia, in April 2005.

SEALED OVER

A boat moored at Newport Beach, California, was sunk in 2005 when 40 invading sea lions piled on to it!

STEERING DOOR

When a Russian yacht lost its rudder in the Southern Ocean in 2005, the clever and resourceful crew used a cabin door as a replacement.

PEDALED CROSSING

In 1992, Kenichi Horie, of Japan, managed to steer a pedal boat 4,660 mi (7,500 km) from Hawaii to Japan. His pedal-powered voyage took him 3½ months.

TOUR OF AMERICA
Don Boehly, of Grayson, Kentucky, set off in September 2004 aiming to cycle through the 50 U.S. states. He expects to complete the 25,000-mi (40,000-km) trip in 2007.

CHIN UP
In December 2003, David Downes, of Felixstowe, England, balanced an open ironing board on his chin for 3 minutes 32 seconds.

GENEROUS DONOR
Frank Loose, of Germany, donates blood every week and has given more than 800 times.

CRAZY GOLF
When Dave Graybill said he was off for a round of golf in 2003, he wasn't planning on playing any ordinary course. The Glendale, Arizona, firefighter had designed a golf course 4,080 mi (6,566 km) long that would take him right across the U.S. The first tee was on Santa Monica Pier, California, and the 18th hole was in Central Park, New York. The round took seven months, through 16 states, and incorporated some of the best-known U.S. landmarks. He hit balls through deserts, across rivers, down streets, and even out of an airplane!

SHARP PRACTICE
Red Stuart, from Philadelphia, Pennsylvania, swallowed 25 swords at once in September 2005! The result of years of training, his intake consisted of a 32-in (80-cm) long broadsword plus 24 smaller swords 18 in (46 cm) in length.

WHEELBARROW PUSH
In 1975, Rev. Geoffrey Howard, a priest from Manchester, England, took 93 days to push a Chinese sailing wheelbarrow 2,000 mi (3,218 km) across the Sahara Desert.

SADDLE WEARY
In April 2005, Randy Davisson, from Decatur, Alabama, succeeded in his mission to ride the same horse in every state in the U.S. and in each Canadian province and territory. The quest, on his faithful appaloosa Eli Whitney, took Randy nearly 5 years to complete and finished when he climbed into the saddle on the island of Oahu, in Hawaii.

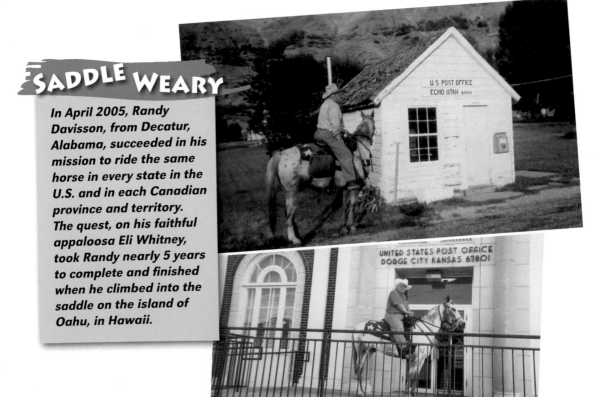

UP AND DOWN

Robert Magniccari, of Rockaway, New Jersey, made 190 take-offs and landings in 24 hours at two airports in New Jersey.

MY LEFT FOOT

When Tad Lietz, from Appleton, Wisconsin, plays the cello, it is a considerable achievement— not only because he's an accomplished cellist, but also because he is missing his left arm and bows instead with his left foot.

WHEELIE FAST

In March 2005, Australia's Matt Mingay reached an incredible speed of 140 mph (225 km/h) doing a motorbike wheelie over a distance of 0.6 mi (1 km) at Temora Aerodrome, New South Wales.

SPINNING STUNT

Australia's R.J. Brunow performed 64 consecutive 360-degree spins (donuts) in a Holden Gemini car at Queensland Raceway in May 2005. He destroyed a brand new set of tires in the process.

SUPER-FIT

In June 2005, at Hartford, Connecticut, Bill Kathan Jr., from Vermont, became the first person in the world to do more than 100 backhanded push-ups in one minute. "Wild Bill," as he is known, proved he was super-fit by performing 109 backhanded push-ups in the 60-second limit.

NAIL SUSPENSION

Harley Newman can suspend himself on just four nails—a variation on the normal bed of nails. Nothing seems to faze him. The U.S. performer can pick combination locks with his teeth by feeling the numbers with his tongue, and has had concrete blocks broken on his face with a sledgehammer. He has also supported a 1,700-lb (771-kg) human pyramid while lying on a bed of nails, and can even escape from a quarter of a mile of plastic food wrap, while holding his breath.

HOUSE HOLE

A family in Waihi, New Zealand, escaped without injury after their house fell into a hole 50 ft (15 m) wide in the middle of the night!

LUCKY NUMBERS

Kris Wilson spends two hours a day writing numbers on notepads as part of his ultimate goal to become the first person in the world to write by hand every number

from one to a million. Wilson, from Provo, Utah, began his challenge in February 2004. Eighteen months later he had reached nearly 600,000. His numbers are for sale— people buy anniversary and birthday numbers, and get a certificate signed by "Mr. Million" himself.

BABY WALKER

Believe it or not, a four-year-old Chinese girl can walk 300 ft (91 m) along a tightrope, suspended 100 ft (30 m) above ground level! Yin Feiyan, from Anhui province, has been tightrope walking since she was two.

DANCING FEET

U.S. entertainer David Meenan managed to tap dance 32 mi (52 km) in 7½ hours at Red Bank, New Jersey, in October 2001.

ANCIENT WHEEL

Archeologists in Slovenia have discovered a wheel that is between 5,100 and 5,350 years old—it is believed to be the oldest ever found.

BACK FLIP

Josh Tenge, from Incline Village, Nevada, performed a back flip measuring 44 ft 10 in (13.7 m) in length on a sandboard in 2000.

JUMPING GRANNY

Thelma Tillery believes in keeping her word. She promised her grandson that she would make a parachute jump when she turned 85, so she did just that. In September 2005, the skydiving grandmother landed safely at Kearney, Nebraska.

FJORD RESCUE

Inge Kavli, age 73, dove into a fjord in Norway and swam out 66 ft (20 m) to rescue a baby boy after his mother accidentally crashed her car into the water.

HIGH-UP KITTY

Bob Dotzauer, a teacher in Cedar Rapids, Iowa, managed to balance a cat in a basket on top of a ladder some 24 ft (7.3 m) tall, while balancing it on his chin!

PAINTBALL WIZARD

Australian martial-arts expert Anthony Kelly, has such quick reactions that he can catch flying arrows and punch faster than Muhammad Ali in his prime—as well as catch speeding paintballs blindfold.

How did you first develop your quick reactions?

"I grew up watching martial-arts star Bruce Lee and boxer Muhammad Ali and was fascinated by how fast people could move. I have trained all over the world and have black belts in seven martial arts. I developed the world's first electronic device for testing reaction speeds, based on a traditional Chinese wooden dummy. My reaction time was under three hundredths of a second."

When did you start to catch things?

"In 1999, I saw an old kung-fu movie where the hero had to catch an arrow. I learned how to do this within a week. I can now catch 38 arrows from three archers in two minutes at a distance of eight meters."

How did you get the idea to catch paintballs?

"A student at my martial-arts center in Armidale, New South Wales, owned a paintball field. He said 'Okay, you can do arrows, how about paintballs?' My record now stands at 28 caught unbroken at 20 meters in 2 minutes, and 11 caught blindfold in the same conditions."

How dangerous is it?

"They shoot the paintballs through a paintball gun at a minimum speed of 240 feet per second—around 70 balls in two minutes. They're really painful, like a cricket ball coming at you at speed, and when I go for a record I'm black and blue. Once an arrow nearly went through my head—it took everything I had to block it. It's stupid to do it, I guess."

Do you have a special technique?

"I'm very in tune with sound. I can get a stopwatch and tell you if it is two or three hundredths of a second between the beeps. So when I catch paintballs blindfold, I can tune into the noise and then bring the ball toward me, slowing its velocity down in milliseconds."

How fast can you punch?

"I hold the record for most punches in one minute, which is 347, and the most in one hour, which is 11,856. I punch on average ten punches per second—Bruce Lee could supposedly do eight, Muhammad Ali six or seven."

How do you train?

"Every day I do crazy things, like trying to slide into a shop door as it's closing. My diet is quite strange in that I eat only meat and potatoes and have never eaten fruit or vegetables—I don't know if that makes a difference!"

Do you use your skills in other areas?

"I travel the world doing TV appearances of my skills, and am the world's leading reaction training coach. I am also a full-time martial arts instructor."

Do you have any future projects?

"I'm working on how fast the body can go. I have taken the old martial-arts stunt of breaking a board one step further—I suspend three boards together, and can break the middle board while the outside boards stay intact. Experts can't work out how! The old masters believed noise could implode human organs, but that's a difficult one to test—so far I'm sticking to breaking balloons!"

HAIR-RAISING

SEW CLEVER!

Despite being unable to use her arms and legs, American Sapna Goel still manages to paint and sew unassisted. Sapna, who contracted polio when young, has developed the amazing ability to thread a sewing needle using her tongue.

IN REVERSE

American Steve Gordon unicycled backward for an amazing 68 mi (109 km) in Springfield, Missouri, in June 1999.

LIVING UNDERWATER

Two Italian divers spent 10 days living underwater in September 2005. Stefano Barbaresi and Stefania Mensa endured cold, fatigue, and, ironically, dehydration to live at a depth of 26 ft (8 m) on the seabed off the island of Ponza, Italy. They slept beneath bedframes, which were turned upside down to stop the sleeper floating upward, and spent most of their time in their underwater "house," which contained two sofas, an exercise bike, books, and a waterproofed television.

Joseph Green, from Brooklyn, New York, was known as "the man with iron hair." His hair was so strong that he could use it to bend an iron bar.

BACKWARD BIKER

Roger Riddell, from Charlotte, North Carolina, jumped over six cars while facing backward on his Harley Davidson motorcycle, in the town of Yakima, Washington State, in 2003.

HIGH JUMP

New Zealander A.J. Hackett jumped 764 ft (233 m) from the Macau Tower on August 17, 2005. He is estimated to have hit speeds of more than 95 mph (150 km/h) during the 20-second descent. Hackett was tied on to a special cable that dramatically slowed his rate of descent once he was just 33 ft (10 m) above the ground, to allow for a safe landing.

Acknowledgments

FRONT COVER (t/l) Randy and Mary Ellen Davisson, (c/l) Dennis Rogers; 4 (l) Dennis Rogers, (r) Randy and Mary Ellen Davisson; 7 Terje Eggum/Scanpix/Camera Press; 8 Photograph by Camera Press; 9 Joe Bowen; 11 Reuters/Michaela Rehle; 13 Reuters/China Daily Information Corp-CDIC; 14–15 Erik Aeder/AP/PA Photos; 16–17 DPA Deutsche Press-Agentur/DPA/PA Photos; 19 AP/AP/Press Association Images; 22 Reuters/China Daily China Daily Information Corp - CDIC; 23 Odd Andersen/AFP/Getty Images; 24–25 Georges Christen; 26 Reuters/China Daily Information Corp-CDIC; 27 Lucas Dawson/Getty Images; 29 (t) Reuters/China Daily Information Corp-CDIC; 30–31 Reuters/China Daily Information Corp-CDIC; 32 Dennis Rogers; 35 Reuters/Michaela Rehle; 36–37 Stevie Star/Mike Malley; 38–39 Reuters/Sergio Moraes; 40 Randy and Mary Ellen Davisson; 41 Bob Child/AP/PA Photos; 42 James Keivom/Getty Images; 44–45 Christine Shing-Kelly

KEY t = top, b = bottom, c = center, l = left, r = right, sp = single page, dp = double page

All other photos are from Ripley's Entertainment Inc.
Every attempt has been made to acknowledge correctly and contact copyright holders and we apologize in advance for any unintentional errors or omissions, which will be corrected in future editions.